**Stacking Silver in the UK – Prote
Age of Inflation** is the definitive gu
who want to safeguard their wealth w

This comprehensive 100,000+ word handbook covers everything from understanding spot price and premiums to buying strategies, secure storage, testing authenticity, community trading, and long-term wealth planning. Written in clean UK English, it's designed to feel approachable yet authoritative, whether you're a beginner or an experienced stacker.

You'll discover:

- The unique challenges and opportunities of stacking silver in the UK

- How inflation and currency weakness erode the pound, and how silver counters it

- The best places to buy silver in Britain, from trusted dealers to peer-to-peer groups

- Testing, storage, and security essentials to protect your stack

- Long-term strategies to pass silver on as generational wealth

Silver has preserved wealth for centuries. In a time of rising inflation and economic uncertainty, this book shows how British investors can use it to build resilience and financial security.

Disclaimer

This book has been created for educational and informational purposes only. It is not intended as financial advice. I am not a financial adviser, and nothing in these pages should be taken as a recommendation to buy, sell or hold any investment. Readers should always conduct their own research and, where necessary, consult a qualified financial professional before making investment decisions.

Artificial intelligence was used as a tool to help research, draft and structure the material presented in this book. Every effort has been made to ensure accuracy and clarity, but errors or omissions may still occur. The author accepts no liability for financial decisions made on the basis of this content.

By continuing to read, you acknowledge that you are responsible for your own financial choices and outcomes.

Chapter 1 – Understanding Silver as an Asset

The Timeless Allure of Silver

Silver has always fascinated human societies. Unlike iron which built empires or copper which drove early tools, silver's importance lies in its unique combination of rarity, beauty and utility. It shines with a brilliance unmatched by other metals, it resists corrosion and it is relatively scarce in the earth's crust. These qualities made silver highly desirable long before modern financial systems were born.

Archaeological finds reveal that as early as 3000 BC, silver was being mined and fashioned into ornaments, vessels and primitive ingots. Ancient Mesopotamian records describe silver being used as a medium of exchange, measured by weight rather than by coins. In many early societies, a fixed weight of silver was accepted as payment for goods or labour, often referred to as "shekels" or similar standards.

Britain's own relationship with silver is deep-rooted. The Roman occupation brought large quantities of silver coinage to the islands, much of it mined from Spanish provinces. After the Romans withdrew, silver retained its role in commerce. The Anglo-Saxons produced some of the most beautiful silver coinage of the early medieval period, their pennies finely struck with kings' portraits and intricate patterns. These coins circulated widely and were trusted because of their consistent silver content.

For centuries, ordinary transactions in Britain relied on silver, not gold. While the wealthy might accumulate gold for large trades, dowries or international settlements, it was silver that moved through markets, fairs and households. Its role as "the people's money" persisted for generations.

This historical connection matters today because it reminds investors that silver has always been more than a shiny trinket. It has served as a practical tool for exchange, a store of wealth in uncertain times and a physical representation of trust. The enduring allure of silver comes not only from its brilliance but from its proven record as money and as wealth.

Silver as Money in British History

The British monetary system owes much to silver. The English penny, introduced under King Offa of Mercia in the late eighth century, was struck almost entirely from silver. This coin became the bedrock of English currency for hundreds of years, circulating throughout markets, villages and towns. Remarkably, for centuries the penny retained a stable weight of silver, which made it one of the most reliable currencies in Europe.

During the medieval period, vast quantities of silver flowed into Britain, much of it mined from continental Europe. The demand for silver coinage was so strong that mints worked continuously to supply the kingdom. Unlike today's inflationary paper notes, the value of these coins rested directly on their silver content. If you held ten pennies, you literally held a certain weight of silver in your hand.

The Tudor era illustrates both the strength and fragility of silver-based money. Henry VIII's extravagant spending on wars, palaces and court life led to the infamous "Great Debasement." Between 1544 and 1551, the silver content of English coinage was drastically reduced, with base metals substituted to stretch royal finances. People quickly noticed that the new coins looked duller and weighed less. Public confidence collapsed and prices rose sharply — an early lesson in inflation driven by currency manipulation.

Elizabeth I later restored confidence by reintroducing higher-quality silver coinage, recognising that trust in money depended on its substance. This episode offers a timeless lesson: debased money loses its purchasing power while honest silver retains it.

The Industrial Revolution and the expansion of global trade in the eighteenth and nineteenth centuries shifted Britain towards a gold standard. Gold became the official anchor of sterling, reflecting Britain's economic might and vast colonial networks. Yet silver remained significant. Millions of silver coins — shillings, florins and half-crowns — circulated in daily life. Silver was practical for transactions too small to involve gold, which kept it rooted in the pockets of ordinary Britons.

The twentieth century saw silver's decline as circulating money. In 1920, the silver content of British coinage was reduced from 92.5% (sterling silver) to 50%. After the Second World War, in 1947, silver was removed entirely, replaced by cupronickel. From that moment, silver ceased to be everyday money in Britain.

Yet the legacy remained. Generations had used silver coins to buy bread, clothing and tools. Many families still remember grandparents passing down silver shillings or crowns as keepsakes. Even now, British silver coins minted before 1947 carry both historical and intrinsic value, treasured by collectors and stackers alike.

This history is crucial for modern investors. It demonstrates that silver has always been tied to the real economy. While governments may change monetary systems, the underlying value of silver itself endures. When currencies falter or policies debase money, silver stands firm as a tangible store of wealth.

Silver in the Modern World

In today's world, silver no longer circulates as daily money but it has taken on new significance. It is simultaneously a precious metal and an industrial commodity.

Silver as a Precious Metal
Investors continue to buy silver in the form of coins, bars and rounds. Modern bullion coins like the Silver Britannia are

produced annually by the Royal Mint, carrying a face value but sold at prices tied to the silver market. Their appeal lies in recognisability, trust and — crucially for UK investors — exemption from Capital Gains Tax when sold at a profit.

Bars and rounds, though not legal tender, are equally popular. Investors who prioritise weight over collectability often choose bars, which can range from small one-ounce ingots to hefty five-kilo blocks. Rounds, privately minted discs of silver, offer another low-cost way to accumulate ounces.

Collectible silver coins add a further dimension. Limited mintage issues, proofs and themed releases attract both stackers and numismatists though they often carry higher premiums. Some investors enjoy mixing bullion stacking with occasional collector purchases, balancing affordability with enjoyment.

Silver as an Industrial Metal

Silver's role in modern industry is immense. Its high electrical and thermal conductivity, anti-bacterial properties and reflectivity make it indispensable.

- Electronics: every smartphone, laptop and tablet contains trace amounts of silver in its circuits.

- Solar panels: silver paste is used in photovoltaic cells, a sector that has grown rapidly as nations invest in renewable energy.

- Medicine: silver's anti-microbial qualities make it valuable in wound dressings, coatings and medical instruments.

- Vehicles: with the rise of electric cars, silver is increasingly used in batteries, sensors and wiring.

Unlike gold which is almost always recycled, a significant proportion of silver used industrially is lost forever. Tiny amounts dispersed across millions of devices are uneconomic to recover. This creates a steady drain on global supply which can tighten markets over time.

The Dual Nature of Silver
This blend of precious and industrial demand makes silver unique. Gold is overwhelmingly monetary while base metals like copper are purely industrial. Silver straddles both worlds. It responds to investor fears about inflation and currency weakness yet its long-term demand is also underpinned by technology and industry.

For UK investors, this duality is important. It means silver prices are influenced by factors beyond the financial markets. A surge in solar energy investment or electronics manufacturing can support prices even if investor sentiment is flat. Conversely, during recessions, industrial demand may soften, amplifying volatility.

Why Investors Turn to Silver

Every generation of investors rediscovers silver for its own reasons. Some are drawn by history, some by affordability and others by its unique position between precious and industrial use. In the UK today, the main motivations can be grouped into a handful of clear themes.

Hedge against inflation

The pound has been losing purchasing power for decades. Wages and savings rarely keep pace with rising living costs and the recent surges in energy and food prices have reminded households how fragile currency-based wealth can be. Silver, by contrast, is finite and tangible. When money is devalued through inflation, hard assets such as silver often hold their ground. Holding a modest stack of silver coins or bars can preserve value in a way that a savings account earning 1% interest never could.

Diversification

The old phrase "don't put all your eggs in one basket" applies to investing as much as to farming. A portfolio made up entirely of equities or property is vulnerable to sector-specific downturns. Silver behaves differently. Its price drivers are distinct from those of the stock market and although it has its own volatility, it provides balance. When one asset class struggles, silver may rise or at least act as a stabiliser.

Affordability compared to gold
 Gold commands respect but also carries a high price tag. At more than £2,000 per ounce, buying even a single ounce of gold is a significant decision. Silver, at a much lower entry point, is accessible to anyone who can set aside £30–£40 at a time. This makes it the natural entry metal for new investors. It allows for regular accumulation, building a position month by month without straining the household budget.

Industrial demand
 Gold's primary use is as jewellery or investment. Silver, on the other hand, is consumed by industry. From solar energy to electric vehicles, demand for silver is growing. This industrial appetite provides a long-term underpinning to the market. Even if investor sentiment wanes for a time, manufacturers will continue to need silver.

Historical precedent
 History shows that silver has endured when paper promises have not. Empires have risen and fallen, governments have come and gone yet silver retains value. It has been used to pay soldiers, settle debts and support economies for millennia. This continuity reassures investors that silver is not a passing trend but a proven store of wealth.

Silver Versus Paper Assets

To appreciate silver's role in a modern portfolio, it helps to compare it directly with mainstream assets available to UK investors.

- **Equities:** shares in companies can grow in value and provide dividends but they rely on the health of corporate earnings and the wider economy. They also carry market risk — sharp downturns can wipe out years of gains.

- **Bonds:** government and corporate bonds promise fixed income but their real return can be eroded by inflation. Rising interest rates also reduce their value.

- **Property:** bricks and mortar are highly prized in Britain and property has historically delivered long-term growth. Yet property is illiquid, requires maintenance and is exposed to policy changes such as taxation or regulation.

- **Cash:** holding cash provides safety and liquidity but is punished by inflation. Every year, the pound buys a little less.

Silver is different from all of these because it is tangible, portable and independent of any institution. A bar of silver in your safe does not depend on a bank, company or government staying solvent. It cannot default or go bankrupt. Its value derives from its substance, not from a promise written on paper.

That is not to say paper assets are worthless. They have their roles and a balanced portfolio may include all of them. But silver provides what they cannot: independence from the financial system. In an era of digital money and mounting debt, many find comfort in knowing that part of their wealth exists outside the reach of banks and bureaucrats.

Price Volatility and Opportunity

No honest discussion of silver would ignore its volatility. Prices can move sharply, both up and down. For some investors, this is off-putting. They want steady, predictable returns and silver does not always deliver them in the short term.

Yet volatility cuts both ways. A metal that can drop 10% in a month can also rise 10%. For disciplined investors, swings create opportunity. By purchasing regularly, regardless of price — a strategy known as pound-cost averaging — you smooth out the bumps. Over time, you build an average cost that reflects both highs and lows and you avoid the trap of trying to time the market.

This approach has proven effective for many UK stackers. A monthly purchase of £100, whether silver is cheap or dear, slowly grows into a meaningful stack. When silver eventually rallies, those who have quietly accumulated are well placed to benefit.

Another opportunity arises from the relationship between silver and gold, known as the gold-to-silver ratio. Historically, this ratio fluctuates and when silver becomes especially cheap relative to gold, some investors swap gold for silver or vice versa to maximise holdings. While this requires careful timing, it shows how volatility can be harnessed rather than feared.

For the patient, silver's volatility is a feature, not a flaw. It allows disciplined investors to acquire ounces when sentiment is low, often at prices that later prove to be bargains.

The UK Investor's Landscape

Investing in silver in Britain comes with specific considerations that distinguish it from other markets.

VAT

Unlike investment gold, silver attracts 20% VAT when bought new from UK dealers. This adds significantly to the purchase price and is often the first shock for newcomers. For example, if the spot price of silver is £20 per ounce and the dealer adds a £5 premium, VAT pushes the price to £30. That is a 50% uplift on spot. Understanding this is vital before making a first purchase.

Capital Gains Tax

One advantage balances the VAT challenge. Certain silver coins, specifically those minted by the Royal Mint with legal tender status — such as the Britannia or the Lunar series — are exempt from Capital Gains Tax for UK residents. This means that if their value increases and you sell at a profit, you do not owe HMRC a penny. For larger stackers, this exemption can make a significant difference.

Dealer choice

Britain benefits from a competitive dealer market. Well-established names like Chards, Atkinsons and BullionByPost alongside smaller independents offer a range of products. Pricing, delivery speed and customer service vary, so it pays to compare. Some dealers specialise in low premiums, others in collectable coins.

Community trading

Because of VAT, many investors turn to the secondary market. Peer-to-peer platforms and communities allow buying and selling between individuals, often at lower prices. Trust and verification are essential but the savings can be substantial. Communities also provide knowledge, camaraderie and opportunities to learn from experienced stackers.

These features combine to create a uniquely British landscape for silver investing. Challenges exist but so do opportunities. With a little education and care, the UK stacker can navigate the market effectively and build a strong position.

The Psychological Dimension of Silver

Beyond numbers and charts, silver offers something intangible: reassurance. Holding physical metal gives a sense of security that digital wealth cannot match. The weight of a coin or bar in your palm feels real in a way that digits on a bank statement never do. This tangibility matters, especially during times of financial uncertainty.

Stacking silver also instils discipline. Regular purchasing, careful storage and diligent record-keeping become habits. Over years, the stack grows steadily, providing both financial and psychological comfort. For many British investors, stacking is more than an investment strategy. It becomes a way of life, a quiet act of independence from a system they do not fully trust.

Silver and Generational Wealth

Historically, families passed down precious metals through generations. Silverware, coins and heirloom jewellery often represented condensed wealth, surviving when paper assets evaporated. For today's investors, stacking silver can serve the same purpose. A carefully built collection of bullion coins or bars can form part of a family's long-term legacy, bridging generations in tangible form.

A silver Britannia tucked away today may one day be handed to a grandchild, its value preserved and perhaps multiplied. Unlike paper savings, which can be eroded by inflation or banking crises, physical silver endures. For families who think long term, silver becomes not just a hedge but a heritage.

Conclusion of Chapter 1

Silver's story in Britain is long and distinguished. From medieval pennies to modern Britannias, from royal mints to online dealers, it has remained both money and commodity. For the modern UK investor, silver offers inflation protection, diversification, affordability and tangible security.

It is not without challenges — volatility, VAT and the need for secure storage — but these can be managed. The appeal of silver lies not in quick profits but in steady accumulation and the reassurance of holding a finite, enduring asset.

As we move into the next chapter, we will examine the mechanics of the silver market itself: spot prices, premiums and how to interpret what you are really paying when you buy silver in the UK.

Chapter 2 – Spot Price and Premiums Explained

The Meaning of Spot Price

Every conversation about silver begins with the spot price. This is the price of silver traded on global markets, quoted per troy ounce. It reflects the wholesale cost of raw silver in large quantities, traded between institutions, refiners and bullion banks.

Spot is constantly moving, updated minute by minute as markets open across London, New York and Asia. For UK investors checking prices online, it usually appears in pounds, though most international charts quote in dollars. The important point is that spot represents a benchmark, not a guaranteed purchase price for an individual buying a handful of coins.

Understanding spot is vital. It anchors expectations and allows investors to judge whether they are paying a fair premium. When a dealer advertises a coin at £35 while spot sits at £29.50, that £5.50 difference is the premium. Without awareness of spot, a newcomer could easily mistake a fair deal for a rip-off or, worse, overpay without knowing it.

How Spot Price Is Set

Spot is not pulled from thin air. It is shaped by global trading across futures contracts, over-the-counter transactions and supply-and-demand dynamics.

- **Futures markets:** much of the world's silver pricing comes through exchanges like COMEX in New York. Traders buy and sell contracts representing large amounts of silver, and their activity sets the tone for the spot market.

- **Physical supply and demand:** mining output, industrial use and investment demand all filter through. A surge in solar panel production or a drop in mining output can nudge prices.

- **Currency fluctuations:** since silver is quoted globally in dollars, the pound-dollar exchange rate matters. A weak pound makes silver more expensive for UK buyers, even if the global dollar price has not moved.

The London Bullion Market Association (LBMA) also plays a role by publishing a daily reference price known as the London Fix. While slightly different from the tick-by-tick spot price, it serves as a reference point for contracts and settlements.

Premiums Explained

Premiums are the extra costs added on top of spot. They reflect the reality of minting, distribution, dealer overheads and, in the UK, taxes. While spot is a global figure, premiums are local and highly variable.

Typical premium components include:

- **Minting and fabrication costs:** turning raw silver into a coin or bar involves design, pressing, finishing and packaging.

- **Dealer margins:** dealers must cover staff, storage, shipping and profit.

- **VAT:** in Britain, silver bullion attracts 20% VAT when bought new. This is applied after the premium, inflating the final cost further.

- **Market demand:** when demand spikes — during financial scares or supply squeezes — premiums rise. A Britannia that normally sells £5 over spot may suddenly cost £8 or £10 above spot if everyone rushes to buy.

For example:

- Spot price = £29.50

- Premium = £5.50

- Subtotal = £35.00

- VAT (20%) = £7.00

- **Final price = £42.00 per ounce**

This simple breakdown shows why many newcomers gasp at their first silver quote. Spot might be under £30, but the actual coin in hand costs more than £40. Awareness of this distinction is essential.

Examples from UK Dealers

Premiums vary between products and sellers. Looking at a few typical cases illustrates the range.

- **1oz Silver Britannia:** usually carries one of the lowest premiums, around £4–£6 over spot before VAT. Its legal tender status and CGT exemption add further appeal.

- **1oz generic rounds:** slightly cheaper than Britannias, sometimes only £3–£4 over spot. However, they lack CGT exemption and recognisability.

- **10oz or 1kg bars:** larger bars reduce fabrication costs per ounce, so premiums shrink. A 1kg bar might only be £2–£3 over spot per ounce.

- **Proof coins or collectables:** these can be £20–£30 above spot or more, reflecting rarity, packaging and collector demand.

Comparing across dealers matters. Cardiff Gold, Chards, Atkinsons and BullionByPost each position themselves differently. Some undercut on basic bullion, others specialise in numismatic or limited-run issues. Savvy investors often check several sites before making a purchase, sometimes within the same day if premiums are moving quickly.

The Effect of VAT

VAT is the single greatest hurdle for UK silver stackers. At 20%, it turns a reasonable premium into a hefty final price. A coin priced £35 before tax becomes £42 with VAT, instantly reducing the investor's head start.

This situation is unique compared to many other countries. In the United States, for example, silver bullion purchases are often exempt from sales tax, depending on the state. In Germany, silver coins used to enjoy reduced VAT rates.

Britain stands out for taxing silver as though it were a luxury rather than an investment.

Because of this, many UK stackers seek ways around VAT:

- **Secondary market:** buying from other individuals avoids VAT, since tax is only levied on new products. Peer-to-peer groups, local meets and online communities offer opportunities.

- **Auctions and fairs:** estate sales and coin fairs sometimes provide silver below dealer prices.

- **European dealers:** some investors order from EU sellers where VAT is structured differently, though Brexit has complicated shipping and customs.

Understanding VAT's impact is vital. It shapes strategy, pushes investors towards certain products (like Britannias for their CGT benefit) and makes the secondary market especially attractive.

Recognising Fair Premiums

The key skill for a silver investor is judging whether a premium is fair. Spot alone does not tell the whole story, and premiums vary with circumstances. A few guidelines help:

- **Low-premium bullion:** around £4–£6 over spot for coins, £2–£3 for bars.

- **High-demand spikes:** premiums can double in panics. Paying £8–£10 over spot for a Britannia during a rush may still be fair if alternatives are sold out.

- **Collectables:** premiums here are subjective. A proof coin at £25 over spot might be reasonable if the mintage is low, but investors should buy such pieces for enjoyment, not pure stacking.

Stackers often develop a rule of thumb: focus on ounces, minimise premiums and avoid emotional purchases unless buying for fun. This discipline keeps the cost basis manageable and maximises the potential return if silver prices rise.

Spot Versus Reality

A frequent frustration for beginners is the gap between the quoted spot price and the real purchase price. It can feel like a trick, as though dealers inflate prices unfairly. In truth, the system is simply layered. Spot is wholesale. Premiums, minting costs and VAT are unavoidable frictions.

This gap also means that silver prices must rise significantly before profits appear. If you pay £42 for a coin when spot is £29.50, you need spot to rise well above £35 before you break even on resale. For long-term stackers this is acceptable, as the horizon is measured in years or decades. Short-term speculators may find it less appealing.

Accepting this reality is part of maturing as a silver investor. Spot is the foundation, but the true cost includes premiums and taxes. Once understood, it ceases to be a shock and instead becomes part of the strategy.

The Role of Supply and Demand

Premiums also reflect supply and demand. When mints produce plenty of coins and investor interest is calm, premiums shrink. During crises, they expand.

The 2020 pandemic offers a vivid example. As financial markets panicked, silver demand surged. Dealers across the UK sold out of Britannias, bars and even high-premium collectables. Premiums doubled or trebled overnight. Buyers were paying £45–£50 for coins that normally cost £35. Yet many accepted it, preferring to secure metal rather than miss out.

This dynamic teaches two lessons. First, buying steadily during calm times prevents panic buying when supplies vanish. Second, premiums themselves can be an indicator of sentiment. Rising premiums often reveal demand before spot moves significantly.

Dealer Practices

Not all dealers operate the same way. Some quote prices inclusive of VAT, others add it at checkout. Some offer free delivery over certain order sizes, while others build shipping into the premium.

Reputable UK dealers usually update prices several times per day to track spot. Others adjust only once daily, which can work in the investor's favour if spot dips after the update. Bulk discounts also matter. Buying ten Britannias may reduce the premium by 50p or £1 per coin compared to buying a single piece.

Because of these variations, experienced stackers rarely buy from the same dealer every time. They keep accounts with several, check prices regularly and pounce when opportunities arise. This competitive approach maximises ounces for each pound spent.

Conclusion of Chapter 2

Spot price is the heartbeat of the silver market, but it is only the beginning. For UK investors, premiums and VAT transform the simple benchmark into a more complex reality. Understanding these layers equips you to judge deals, avoid overpaying and plan long-term strategies.

While the system may feel stacked against the small investor, knowledge is power. By learning how spot is set, why premiums exist and how VAT shapes the market, British stackers can make informed decisions. The goal is not to chase every penny but to build a steady, disciplined stack at fair prices.

In the next chapter we will explore the forms that silver takes — coins, bars and rounds — and how to choose the right mix for your own stacking strategy.

Chapter 3 – Types of Silver for UK Stackers

The Variety of Silver Products

One of the first decisions a UK stacker faces is what form of silver to buy. Dealers offer coins, bars and rounds, each with advantages and drawbacks. Beyond these, there are collectable proofs, commemoratives and even poured or hand-crafted pieces. Choosing the right mix depends on budget, goals and personal preference.

Newcomers often ask, "What is the best type of silver to start with?" The answer is not the same for everyone. A young stacker building ounces on a tight budget may focus on the lowest cost per gram, while someone interested in passing wealth to family might prioritise recognisable government coins. Collectors with an eye for design may enjoy proofs, even at higher premiums.

Understanding each type of silver in detail allows you to make informed decisions.

Bullion Coins

Bullion coins are minted by national mints with a face value and legal tender status, although their true worth lies in their metal content.

The Silver Britannia

For UK investors, the Silver Britannia is the most important coin. Introduced in 1997, it has become the flagship bullion coin of the Royal Mint. Modern Britannias are struck in 999 fine silver and feature advanced anti-counterfeit security features such as micro-text and radial lines.

What makes Britannias particularly attractive is their exemption from Capital Gains Tax. Because they are legal tender in the UK, any profits on sale are free of CGT. This makes them highly efficient for larger stacks and a staple for British investors.

Other Popular Coins

While Britannias dominate the UK market, many stackers enjoy international coins for variety or global recognisability. Examples include:

- **American Silver Eagle** – the most widely traded silver coin worldwide, recognised everywhere.

- **Canadian Maple Leaf** – valued for its purity and security features.

- **Austrian Philharmonic** – popular across Europe, with a distinctive design.

- **Australian Kangaroo** – a cost-effective bullion coin.

International coins are not CGT-exempt in the UK, but they are trusted worldwide. Some investors like to keep a mix, ensuring flexibility if they ever wish to sell abroad.

Advantages of Coins

- High recognisability and liquidity.

- Government guarantee of weight and purity.

- CGT exemption for Britannias and certain other Royal Mint coins.

Disadvantages of Coins

- Higher premiums compared to bars, especially for small quantities.

- Collectable issues can tempt buyers into overpaying for fancy packaging.

Silver Bars

Bars are the simplest and most efficient way to stack large amounts of silver. They come in sizes from tiny 1g pieces up to 5kg or more. For most UK stackers, the sweet spot is between 100g and 1kg, balancing affordability with decent premiums.

Cast vs Minted Bars

- **Minted bars** are machine-pressed, with sharp edges and polished finishes. They are attractive and consistent, often sealed in assay cards.

- **Cast bars** are poured into moulds, giving a more rugged appearance. They are usually cheaper per ounce and appeal to those who value weight over looks.

Popular Bar Brands in the UK

- **Royal Mint** produces Britannia bars, well respected and often carrying a modest premium.

- **German refiners** such as Heraeus and Umicore are common in the UK market.

- **Swiss refiners** like PAMP and Valcambi are globally recognised.

Advantages of Bars

- Lower premiums, especially in larger sizes.

- Efficient for stacking bulk weight.

- Widely available from UK and European dealers.

Disadvantages of Bars

- Not CGT exempt.

- Large bars can be harder to sell in small portions.

- Less recognisable to the general public than coins.

Silver Rounds

Rounds are privately minted pieces, usually one ounce in size, similar to coins but without legal tender status. They often feature creative designs, ranging from patriotic motifs to fantasy themes.

Why Rounds Appeal

Rounds tend to be cheaper than government coins, making them a cost-effective way to add ounces. They are especially popular in the United States, though less common in the UK. For British stackers, rounds can be an affordable alternative when premiums on coins rise sharply.

Advantages of Rounds

- Lower premiums compared to coins.

- Huge variety of designs for collectors who enjoy artwork.

- Easy to store in tubes, just like coins.

Disadvantages of Rounds

- Not legal tender, so no CGT exemption.

- Recognition is weaker in the UK compared to coins or branded bars.

Proof and Collectable Coins

Not all silver coins are meant for stacking. Proofs and commemoratives are minted with polished dies, frosted details and elaborate packaging. They are aimed at collectors and often come in presentation boxes with certificates.

For stackers, these carry risks. Premiums can be many times spot value, and resale depends on collector demand. A proof coin bought for £100 when spot is £25 may never recover its premium. However, certain limited issues do gain value over time, especially if mintage is low or designs are iconic.

Some investors enjoy mixing a little of this side of the hobby into their stack, treating proofs as both an indulgence and a potential speculative play. The key is moderation: proofs should be the icing on the cake, not the cake itself.

Poured and Hand-Crafted Silver

A niche but growing area of stacking is poured or hand-crafted silver. Small refiners and artisans produce bars and shapes with unique finishes, often stamped by hand. Skulls, hexagons, custom logos and one-off pours attract collectors who enjoy owning something distinctive.

These pieces almost always command higher premiums. They are closer to art than bullion, yet many stackers appreciate the individuality and craftsmanship. While not suitable for building bulk weight, they add character to a collection.

Junk or Pre-Decimal Silver

Another option in the UK is older circulating coinage with silver content.

- **Sterling silver (92.5%)** coins minted before 1920.
- **50% silver coins** minted between 1920 and 1946.

These coins are often referred to as "junk silver" in the US, though in Britain they are usually called pre-decimal or scrap silver. They carry historical interest and sometimes surface in family heirlooms or coin shops.

Premiums vary depending on condition, but these coins can be a low-cost way to add ounces. Their recognisability also makes them easy to shift among fellow collectors.

Choosing the Right Mix

There is no universal formula for what types of silver to hold, but a few guiding principles help.

- **Prioritise recognisability and liquidity.** For UK investors, that means a core of Britannias.

- **Add bars for low-cost weight.** Larger bars reduce premiums and build bulk.

- **Use rounds selectively.** They can be cheaper when dealer premiums on coins spike.

- **Treat proofs and pours as optional extras.** Buy them for enjoyment, not as the foundation of your stack.

- **Consider pre-decimal silver** if you enjoy history or want smaller denominations for potential barter.

Over time, most stackers gravitate towards a blend that suits their goals. Some end up almost exclusively in Britannias, others build shelves of kilo bars, while collectors pepper their stacks with a few proofs or pours for fun. The key is knowing why you are buying and keeping the focus on value.

Conclusion of Chapter 3

The world of silver offers variety to suit every taste. For UK investors, the Silver Britannia stands as the most tax-efficient and recognisable option, while bars provide low-cost bulk. Rounds, proofs and pours add colour for those who enjoy variety, and pre-decimal silver connects modern stackers with history.

There is no wrong way to stack, only choices that align better or worse with your goals. The disciplined investor builds a foundation of efficient bullion, then adds other pieces if desired. With knowledge of each type, you can shape a stack that balances practicality with personal satisfaction.

In the next chapter we will look at **stacking strategies** — from pound-cost averaging to budget planning — and explore how to build a disciplined approach that grows your stack steadily over time.

Chapter 4 – Stacking Strategies

Why Strategy Matters

Silver stacking is deceptively simple: buy silver, hold silver. Yet the approach you take can make the difference between a disciplined, growing stack and a chaotic collection that drains your budget. Without a clear plan, it is easy to overspend, chase collectables, or buy at inopportune moments. With a strategy, every purchase supports your long-term goals.

In the UK, where VAT inflates prices and premiums vary widely, strategy becomes even more important. A well-considered approach helps you maximise ounces for every pound spent, avoid common mistakes, and keep your stacking sustainable over years.

Setting Goals

The first step in building a strategy is defining your goals. Ask yourself why you are stacking silver. Common motivations include:

- **Preserving wealth against inflation.** Silver acts as a hedge when currency weakens.

- **Diversifying investments.** A portion of silver balances equities, property and cash.

- **Preparing for uncertainty.** Some see silver as a form of financial insurance.

- **Building generational wealth.** Silver can be passed down as a tangible legacy.

Your goals will shape your decisions. A wealth preserver may focus heavily on low-premium bullion, while a collector at heart may allow room for proofs and special editions. A long-term planner will prioritise consistency, whereas a speculator may try to time swings in the market.

Budgeting

A sustainable stack depends on a realistic budget. Silver should enhance your finances, not strain them. The most successful stackers decide a fixed monthly amount and stick to it, whether £50 or £500.

Benefits of a fixed budget

- Removes emotion from purchases.

- Builds discipline.

- Smooths volatility by spreading buys across time.

- Keeps personal finances balanced.

Budgeting also prevents the all-too-common mistake of panic buying during price spikes. When silver surges, new stackers often feel compelled to buy heavily, fearing they will miss out. Those with a set budget can step back, stick to their plan, and continue accumulating steadily.

Pound-Cost Averaging

Perhaps the most powerful strategy for UK stackers is pound-cost averaging. This means committing to regular purchases regardless of price. One month silver might be £42 per ounce, the next £36, the next £40. Over time, your average cost smooths out, insulating you from short-term volatility.

This approach requires patience. You may feel frustrated if you buy just before a dip, but the long-term trend of steady accumulation matters more than individual trades. Pound-cost averaging suits anyone with a long horizon and a steady budget.

Weight Stacker, Collector or Hybrid

Stackers often fall into three broad categories.

Weight Stacker
Focused on building as many ounces as possible for the lowest cost. Buys bars and low-premium coins, cares little for design or collectability. For a UK weight stacker, 1kg bars or tubes of Britannias are staples.

Collector
Buys silver for beauty and rarity. Seeks proofs, low-mintage coins and unusual designs. The focus is on enjoyment as much as investment. Collectors may pay high premiums but take pride in their holdings.

Hybrid
Combines both approaches. Maintains a solid core of bullion for wealth preservation, then adds occasional collectables for enjoyment. Many UK stackers fall into this category, striking a balance between efficiency and fun.

Knowing which camp you lean towards helps guide purchases. A weight stacker who finds themselves spending hundreds on proofs may need to reassess. A collector who regrets high premiums may shift towards bullion. Self-awareness keeps your strategy coherent.

Buying in Bulk

Premiums shrink when you buy larger quantities. A single Britannia may cost £6 over spot, but a tube of 25 may reduce that to £5 per coin. A kilo bar spreads minting costs more efficiently than ten 100g bars.

This does not mean you must save thousands before buying. Even small investors can benefit by pooling orders. For example, buying four or five Britannias at once often secures a better rate than purchasing one. Over years, these small savings compound into meaningful extra ounces.

Timing Purchases

Trying to time the market perfectly is a trap. Few succeed consistently. Yet there are ways to make timing work in your favour without falling into speculation.

- **Buy the dips, cautiously.** If silver drops sharply, consider adding a little extra that month.

- **Avoid chasing spikes.** When premiums explode and dealers sell out, stick to your plan.

- **Use ratios.** The gold-to-silver ratio can guide swaps. When silver looks especially cheap relative to gold, some shift weight into silver.

Above all, timing should supplement, not replace, your core plan of steady accumulation.

Secondary Market Strategies

In the UK, the secondary market is vital because of VAT. Buying pre-owned silver avoids the 20% surcharge. Strategies here include:

- **Peer-to-peer trading groups.** Communities allow deals directly between individuals.

- **Coin fairs and shops.** Local events can yield bargains.

- **Auctions.** Estate sales sometimes release bulk silver at attractive prices.

Success in the secondary market depends on trust and verification. Always check weights, use magnets and consider ping tests. Once relationships are built, peer trading can become one of the most cost-effective ways to grow a stack.

Avoiding Common Mistakes

New stackers often learn lessons the hard way. A few pitfalls are worth avoiding from the start:

- **Overpaying for proofs.** A beautiful coin at £100 with £25 of silver content rarely makes financial sense.

- **Neglecting storage.** Stacks left in shoeboxes or drawers risk damage or theft.

- **Impatience.** Expecting quick profits from silver leads to disappointment.

- **Ignoring premiums.** Focusing only on spot without checking the real cost results in poor deals.

- **Selling too soon.** Many regret parting with silver during temporary dips, only to see prices recover.

Building Discipline

Ultimately, stacking silver is about discipline. The metal itself does not generate income or dividends. Its role is long-term preservation. Discipline means:

- Buying steadily, even when excitement fades.

- Resisting hype during speculative manias.

- Storing safely and recording purchases.

- Reviewing progress annually, not daily.

Discipline transforms a scattered collection into a structured stack that can weather decades.

Conclusion of Chapter 4

Stacking silver is simple but not easy. Without strategy, it is easy to overspend, chase collectables or panic during swings. With a plan, silver becomes a steady foundation of wealth.

UK investors face unique challenges such as VAT and fluctuating premiums, but by budgeting, pound-cost averaging and knowing your stacking style, you can overcome them. Focus on consistency, discipline and value, and your stack will grow into something meaningful over time.

In the next chapter we will explore **where to buy silver in the UK** — from established dealers to peer-to-peer markets — and how to choose reliable sources for your purchases.

Chapter 5 – Where to Buy Silver in the UK

The Importance of Trusted Sources

Silver is valuable, portable and easy to counterfeit. Where you buy matters just as much as what you buy. A secure, trustworthy source ensures that your investment is genuine, fairly priced and delivered safely. Choosing the right avenue is one of the most important decisions for a UK stacker.

There are four main routes to acquiring silver: established dealers, the Royal Mint, secondary market trading and international suppliers. Each has advantages and risks. The best approach often combines several sources, giving flexibility and access to the best prices.

Established UK Dealers

Britain has a well-developed bullion market with a handful of respected names that dominate. These dealers sell a wide range of coins and bars, ship securely and provide reassurance through reputation.

Chards
Based in Blackpool, Chards is one of the longest-established precious metals dealers in the country. They are known for competitive pricing, especially on bullion coins like Britannias.

Chards also sell second-hand silver, which avoids VAT, making them popular with experienced stackers.

Atkinsons Bullion
 Operating from Birmingham, Atkinsons has built a strong online presence. Their prices are consistently competitive, and their site is user-friendly. They offer a wide choice of bullion and collectables, with clear pricing inclusive of VAT where applicable.

Cardiff Gold
 A smaller but well-respected dealer, Cardiff Gold is known for personal service and sharp pricing. They frequently stock both new and pre-owned silver, which appeals to budget-conscious stackers looking to avoid VAT when possible.

BullionByPost
 As one of the UK's largest online dealers, BullionByPost benefits from scale. Their website updates prices frequently in line with spot. They are not always the cheapest but they offer fast delivery and reliability, which appeals to beginners who value reassurance.

Other dealers
 Several smaller firms operate online or through shops. Some specialise in numismatic coins, others in large bars. While less known, they can provide excellent service and competitive pricing. The key is to research thoroughly and check customer reviews.

Advantages of established dealers

- Reputable and trusted, reducing the risk of fakes.
- Wide choice of products.
- Clear pricing linked to spot.
- Secure, insured delivery.

Disadvantages of established dealers

- All new silver attracts VAT.
- Premiums vary, and you may pay more for convenience.

The Royal Mint

The Royal Mint holds a unique position. As the official producer of UK currency, its bullion products carry unquestioned legitimacy. Silver Britannias, Lunar coins and Royal Mint bars are staples of the UK market.

Buying directly from the Mint ensures authenticity, but pricing is rarely the best. Premiums tend to be higher than those offered by private dealers, and delivery times can be slower. For many, the Royal Mint is more of a symbolic or one-off purchase source than a regular supplier. Still, some stackers value the direct link to Britain's minting authority.

Advantages

- Absolute assurance of authenticity.
- Products that are CGT-exempt.

Disadvantages

- Premiums higher than many private dealers.
- Delivery can be slower during busy periods.

Secondary Market Trading

Because of VAT, the secondary market is essential for UK stackers. Buying pre-owned silver avoids the 20% surcharge, significantly reducing costs.

Peer-to-peer groups
Online communities provide direct access to fellow investors. Members list coins and bars for sale, often at prices below dealer levels. Trust is key, and reputation within the group matters. Trades are usually done via bank transfer, with postage or meet-ups arranged.

Coin shops and fairs
Although rarer than in the past, some towns still have coin shops that trade bullion. Coin fairs bring together dealers and collectors, where silver often changes hands at competitive prices. The advantage is being able to inspect items before purchase.

Auctions
From eBay to specialist auction houses, silver frequently appears in lots. Bargains are possible, though fees, shipping and the risk of fakes must be considered. Caution and due diligence are vital.

Advantages of the secondary market

- No VAT on pre-owned silver.

- Often lower premiums than dealers.

- Access to discontinued or rare pieces.

Disadvantages of the secondary market

- Requires trust and verification.

- Risk of fakes if dealing with strangers.

- Less consumer protection than established dealers.

International Dealers

Some UK stackers look abroad, especially to Europe, for cheaper silver. Before Brexit, many ordered from German dealers who offered silver coins at reduced VAT rates. Since 2021, customs changes have complicated this, with imports now subject to VAT and potential delays.

Despite this, some still find opportunities, particularly with bulk orders or unique products not widely stocked in Britain. Shipping costs and customs risk must be factored in, and patience is needed for deliveries.

Advantages

- Access to products not common in the UK.

- Potential for lower premiums on certain items.

Disadvantages

- VAT and customs charges may apply.

- Longer shipping times.

- More complex returns or disputes.

Spotting Red Flags

Wherever you buy, it is important to recognise warning signs of unreliable sellers.

- Prices far below market without explanation.

- Lack of clear contact details or company information.

- Poor online reviews or no track record.

- Pressure tactics urging you to "buy now before it is too late."

- Reluctance to provide photographs or details of items.

If in doubt, walk away. The silver market is competitive, and genuine deals are plentiful. It is better to miss one opportunity than to risk buying fakes or losing money to fraud.

Blending Sources

Most UK stackers find that the best approach is to blend several buying avenues. Dealers provide reliability, the secondary market offers VAT-free bargains, and occasional overseas orders diversify the stack. Some stackers use the Royal Mint only for special releases, others rely on it for consistency.

The key is flexibility. Sticking rigidly to one source may mean overpaying. Checking several dealers before buying, monitoring community groups and staying open to auctions or fairs maximises opportunities.

Conclusion of Chapter 5

In the UK, buying silver requires awareness of VAT, dealer practices and the value of the secondary market. Established dealers provide trust and convenience, the Royal Mint ensures authenticity, peer-to-peer trades reduce costs, and overseas orders add variety. Each route has advantages and risks.

By blending sources and remaining vigilant, UK stackers can secure silver efficiently and safely. With trusted supply chains in place, the focus can shift to building strategies for storage, security and long-term management.

In the next chapter we will look at **how to test and verify silver**, ensuring that every coin or bar in your stack is genuine.

Chapter 6 – Testing and Verifying Silver

Why Verification Matters

Silver is a trusted store of value, but that trust is only as strong as the assurance that your metal is genuine. Counterfeit coins and bars exist, often produced with remarkable detail. While most UK stackers will never encounter fakes from reputable dealers, the risk rises when buying on the secondary market or through private trades.

Verification is not about paranoia. It is about peace of mind. Every investor benefits from knowing simple ways to confirm authenticity. The goal is not to become an expert metallurgist but to use straightforward methods that provide confidence.

The Basics of Genuine Silver

Before testing, it helps to know what to expect from real silver.

- **Weight:** bullion coins and bars are produced to precise specifications. A 1oz Britannia should weigh 31.1 grams with very little variation.

- **Dimensions:** genuine coins have consistent diameter and thickness. Deviations suggest tampering.

- **Look and feel:** silver has a distinctive shine, softer than chrome, brighter than steel. It feels cold to the touch and carries noticeable heft for its size.

- **Sound:** when struck gently, silver produces a high, clear ringing tone that base metals struggle to replicate.

Understanding these fundamentals equips you to spot obvious fakes before reaching for advanced tools.

Simple Home Tests

There are several low-cost, non-destructive tests that every UK stacker can learn.

The Magnet Test

Silver is not magnetic. If a coin sticks firmly to a magnet, it is almost certainly fake. However, some counterfeiters use non-magnetic metals such as lead or copper, so a pass does not prove authenticity on its own.

A refinement is the "slide test." Place a coin on a tilted surface with a strong magnet underneath. Real silver falls slowly due to electromagnetic resistance. Other metals slide quickly.

The Ping Test

When balanced on a fingertip and tapped with another coin, silver produces a long, clear ring. Base metals sound dull or short. Many stackers train their ears by comparing known genuine coins to new purchases. Apps can even analyse the sound frequency to confirm results.

The Ice Test

Silver has very high thermal conductivity. Place an ice cube on a silver bar and it begins to melt rapidly. While this is not precise, it demonstrates one of silver's unique properties.

Visual Inspection
A magnifying glass or jeweller's loupe reveals detail. Genuine coins have sharp edges and consistent designs. Blurred features, uneven rims or sloppy details suggest poor quality fakes.

Measuring Tools

Basic equipment increases confidence.

- **Digital scales:** accurate to at least 0.01g, used to confirm weight.

- **Callipers:** measure diameter and thickness to compare with official specifications.

- **Reference charts:** most mints publish dimensions of their bullion coins. Keeping a chart to hand makes comparison easy.

For example, a Britannia should measure 38.61mm in diameter and weigh 31.1g. Any significant deviation raises questions.

Advanced Devices

Serious stackers sometimes invest in more advanced verification tools. These are not essential for beginners but can be worthwhile for those with larger stacks or frequent secondary market trades.

Sigma Metalytics Machine
This device measures electrical resistivity to determine whether an item matches the profile of genuine silver. It works through capsules or packaging, making it non-invasive. A Sigma is not cheap but it offers reassurance for high-value purchases.

XRF Analyser
X-ray fluorescence devices provide detailed analysis of metal composition. They are expensive and mainly used by jewellers, refiners and large dealers. Few private stackers own one, but some communities and fairs may offer access.

Ultrasound or Density Tests
These methods measure how sound or liquid moves through the item, comparing results to expected values for silver. They can detect fakes with a silver coating over a base metal core.

Common Counterfeit Methods

Understanding how fakes are produced helps in spotting them.

- **Plated coins:** base metal discs coated with a thin layer of silver. These usually fail weight or ping tests.

- **Copper or lead cores:** sometimes used to mimic silver's density. Dimensional checks and resistivity tests reveal the difference.

- **High-quality replicas:** modern technology can create convincing copies of popular coins. Buying from trusted dealers is the best defence.

Counterfeiters often target well-known coins like American Eagles, Maple Leafs or even Britannias. Collectable proofs and high-value bars are also imitated.

When to Test

Not every purchase requires exhaustive checks. A coin from a top UK dealer arrives with strong assurance. Still, many stackers enjoy performing a quick magnet or ping test for peace of mind.

The most important times to verify are:

- Buying from private sellers.

- Acquiring unusual or rare items.

- Making large purchases on the secondary market.

Testing becomes second nature. Over time, you develop an instinct for how silver should look, weigh and sound.

Community and Trust

One of the strongest protections against fakes is the stacking community itself. Peer-to-peer groups build reputations, where trusted members become reliable sources of pre-owned silver. Reviews, feedback systems and repeat dealings reduce risk.

In-person meets, coin fairs and collector clubs also provide opportunities to compare notes. Many experienced stackers are happy to demonstrate testing techniques for newcomers. Community knowledge is a powerful safeguard.

Conclusion of Chapter 6

Verification is part science, part habit. A combination of simple tests, measuring tools and trusted sources ensures that your stack is genuine. For most UK investors, digital scales, callipers and a good ear for the ping test are sufficient. Larger stacks may justify advanced devices.

By building confidence in your silver, you protect your wealth and enjoy peace of mind. Counterfeiters exist, but with knowledge and vigilance they pose little threat.

In the next chapter we will explore **storage and security** — how to protect your silver once you have confirmed it is genuine.

Chapter 7 – Storage and Security

Why Storage Matters

Buying silver is only the beginning. Once in your hands, the responsibility of safekeeping begins. Silver is dense, valuable and attractive to thieves. Without a clear storage strategy, your investment risks loss, damage or simply becoming disorganised.

A good storage plan balances three priorities: security, accessibility and discretion. Security protects against theft, accessibility ensures you can reach your silver when needed, and discretion keeps others from knowing you hold it at all.

Home Storage

Most UK stackers store at least part of their silver at home. The benefits are obvious: instant access and full control. Yet home storage requires forethought.

Safes
A proper safe is the foundation of secure storage. Choose one that is fire-resistant, heavy and bolted to the floor or wall. Lightweight safes that can be carried off offer little protection. A safe should be discreetly placed, ideally out of sight of visitors or delivery workers.

Decoy Safes

Some stackers use a two-layer approach. A small, obvious safe holds a token amount of silver, while the main stack rests in a hidden or more secure safe elsewhere. In the unlikely event of a break-in, the decoy may satisfy a thief in a hurry.

Hiding Places

Not all silver needs to sit in a safe. Some scatter small amounts around the house in hidden spots: under floorboards, inside false walls or in containers that blend with ordinary belongings. While creative, these methods should complement, not replace, a proper safe.

Off-Site Storage

For larger stacks, many prefer professional storage solutions.

Bank Safety Deposit Boxes

Although not as common in Britain as elsewhere, some banks still offer safety deposit services. Boxes provide discreet, secure storage, though access is limited to banking hours and rental fees apply.

Specialist Vaults
Private vaulting companies offer storage specifically for bullion. Facilities are often insured and guarded, with 24-hour security systems. Some allow you to view or withdraw your silver by appointment. Costs vary but are typically charged annually by weight.

Advantages of Off-Site Storage

- Professional security reduces theft risk.

- Insurance often included.

- Suitable for very large holdings.

Disadvantages of Off-Site Storage

- Fees reduce long-term returns.

- Limited accessibility.

- Requires trust in the custodian.

Insurance

Regardless of where you store silver, consider insurance. Standard home contents policies may not cover bullion beyond small amounts. Some insurers offer specialist policies for precious metals, though premiums rise with declared value.

Keeping receipts, photographs and a clear record of purchases supports insurance claims. Confidentiality must be balanced with documentation. Store digital records securely, and avoid discussing holdings with those who do not need to know.

Organisation

A growing stack quickly becomes cluttered if not organised. Tubes, capsules and storage boxes protect coins from scratches and tarnish. Bars should be kept in their original packaging when possible.

Many stackers label tubes with purchase dates and prices, making it easy to track cost basis. Larger collections benefit from an inventory spreadsheet recording weight, type, price and location. Organisation not only prevents loss but also helps when selling or passing silver on to heirs.

Tarnish and Care

Silver naturally tarnishes when exposed to air and moisture. While tarnish does not reduce intrinsic value, it may affect resale appeal. To slow tarnish:

- Keep coins in capsules or sealed tubes.

- Store in a dry, stable environment.

- Use anti-tarnish strips or silica gel packs in safes.

Avoid polishing bullion coins, as abrasives reduce value. Proofs or collectables should remain in original capsules, untouched by bare hands. Bars are less sensitive but still benefit from careful handling.

Discretion

Perhaps the most overlooked aspect of storage is discretion. The fewer people who know about your silver, the safer it is. Casual conversations, social media posts or careless mentions can attract unwanted attention. Even among friends, loose talk spreads quickly.

Deliveries should be discreet too. Reputable dealers use plain packaging, but consider directing shipments to secure locations or times when you are available to receive them. Piles of missed delivery cards or packages left on doorsteps undermine security.

Balancing Accessibility and Safety

One challenge of storage is balancing safety with accessibility. Silver stored in a high-security vault is safe but inconvenient if you want to sell quickly. A safe at home provides instant access but carries theft risk. Many UK stackers split their holdings, keeping a core reserve off-site while maintaining a smaller working stack at home.

This approach offers flexibility: off-site storage preserves wealth long term, while home storage allows fast liquidity if an opportunity arises.

Legacy and Inheritance

For long-term investors, silver often becomes part of family legacy planning. Storage should account for what happens if the unexpected occurs. Ensure that trusted family members know where silver is kept and how to access it. Clear records prevent confusion, lost value or disputes.

Some leave instructions with wills or solicitors, detailing holdings without disclosing precise locations publicly. Others involve children early, teaching them about silver so knowledge passes seamlessly.

Conclusion of Chapter 7

Silver's physical nature is both its strength and its challenge. Unlike digital assets, it cannot be hacked or deleted, but it must be physically protected. Home safes, vaults, insurance and careful organisation all contribute to security. Discretion is equally vital, ensuring only those who need to know are aware.

A good storage plan provides peace of mind, allowing you to focus on building your stack rather than worrying about its safety. With silver secure, the next step is to consider how and when to sell — the subject of the next chapter.

Chapter 8 – Selling and Liquidating Silver in the UK

Why Selling Matters

Buying silver is only half the journey. Eventually, every stacker faces the question of how to sell. Some aim to cash out after decades, others trade more frequently, and many view silver as a resource that can be tapped during emergencies. Selling well is as important as buying smart. It determines how much value you recover from your stack and how smoothly the process unfolds.

Timing Your Sale

The first decision is when to sell. Silver prices fluctuate daily and can swing dramatically over months or years. Timing can significantly affect your outcome.

- **Long-term liquidation:** many stackers plan to hold for decades and sell in retirement. The idea is that silver's purchasing power will be preserved or enhanced.

- **Opportunistic selling:** some sell portions when prices spike, taking advantage of temporary surges.

- **Emergency sales:** in times of personal crisis, silver provides liquidity. Selling a few coins can cover urgent expenses without resorting to loans.

Perfect timing is rare. Few manage to sell at exact peaks. The best approach is to know your goals, track the market and avoid panic.

Where to Sell

Several options exist in the UK, each with strengths and weaknesses.

Bullion Dealers
Established dealers such as Chards, Atkinsons, Cardiff Gold and BullionByPost buy silver directly. They usually pay a percentage of spot price, often slightly below the rate at which they sell. Dealers provide reliability and immediate payment, but the spread between buy and sell prices can reduce returns.

Peer-to-Peer Trading
Communities and forums allow private trades. Here, you may achieve better prices by negotiating directly with other stackers. Selling Britannias at £2–£3 over spot, for example, is often possible peer-to-peer. The trade-off is trust: you must manage payment, postage and reputation carefully.

Coin Shops and Fairs
Some high street coin shops still operate, and fairs provide opportunities to sell to collectors and small dealers. Prices vary, and negotiation is part of the process. Proofs and older coins may fetch stronger premiums here than through bullion dealers.

Auctions
Silver is regularly sold at auctions, both online and in physical houses. This method suits collectables or large collections but

comes with buyer fees and seller commissions. For bullion, auctions often yield less predictable results.

Capital Gains Tax Considerations

For UK residents, Capital Gains Tax is an important factor when selling. Profits on silver bars and most foreign coins may be subject to CGT if gains exceed the annual allowance. However, Britannias and certain other Royal Mint coins are exempt.

This makes Britannias not only efficient for buying but also practical for selling. Large stacks of CGT-exempt coins can be liquidated without tax headaches, whereas selling kilo bars at a significant profit may involve paperwork and liabilities.

Selling in Portions

A common mistake is to sell everything at once. Breaking sales into portions spreads risk and ensures liquidity over time.

- **Small lots:** selling tubes of Britannias or single bars keeps demand high and avoids scaring off buyers with bulk sales.

- **Gradual liquidation:** offloading over weeks or months helps capture better prices during swings.

- **Liquidity balance:** selling some while holding some preserves long-term exposure.

This staged approach is particularly valuable for those liquidating in retirement or funding big expenses.

Preparing to Sell

Presentation and organisation affect saleability. Coins kept in capsules or tubes fetch stronger prices than scratched or tarnished pieces. Keeping purchase receipts and an organised inventory builds confidence with buyers.

Photographs are important for online sales. Clear, well-lit images showing both sides of the coin or bar reassure potential buyers. Avoid stock images, which may cause suspicion.

Payment Methods

Safe and reliable payment is crucial.

- **PayPal:** common for peer-to-peer trades, providing quick settlement.

- **Cash:** possible for in-person trades but carries security risks.

- **Bank transfers:** when selling to dealers, payment is usually by bank transfer within a few days.

Avoiding Pitfalls

Selling silver is not without hazards. Common pitfalls include:

- **Rushing:** panic selling during dips locks in losses.

- **Ignoring premiums:** selling only at spot may undervalue coins like Britannias, which command higher resale premiums.

- **Falling for scams:** fake payment confirmations or fraudulent buyers occasionally appear in peer-to-peer settings.

- **Overlooking fees:** auctions and some dealers deduct commission, reducing final returns.

Patience and research prevent most problems.

Emergency Sales

Life is unpredictable. Redundancy, medical bills or urgent expenses may force quick liquidation. This is when silver's liquidity shines. Dealers will always buy, even if not at the highest prices. Having a plan for emergency sales reduces stress. Many stackers keep a small portion of their stack easily accessible for precisely this purpose.

Legacy and Passing On Silver

For stackers thinking long term, silver is often intended for inheritance. Planning for this transition matters. Heirs unfamiliar with bullion may sell hastily at poor prices. Leaving instructions, preferred dealers and an inventory ensures value is preserved. Some even sell part of their stack during later years, converting it into cash or gifts for family, while leaving the remainder as a legacy.

Conclusion of Chapter 8

Selling silver is as strategic as buying it. The UK market offers multiple outlets — from dealers to peer groups — each suited to different circumstances. CGT rules shape decisions, especially for larger stacks. Portioning sales, preparing well and avoiding pitfalls maximise returns.

Silver provides liquidity in emergencies, optionality in retirement and legacy for families. By planning ahead, you ensure that your stack delivers value when you eventually part with it.

In the next chapter we will explore **the role of silver in relation to inflation and purchasing power**, examining how silver protects wealth as the pound declines.

Chapter 9 – Inflation and Purchasing Power

Inflation in Everyday Life

For most people in Britain, inflation is felt not in economic reports but in the supermarket aisle, at the petrol station or on utility bills. Over decades, the pound has consistently lost purchasing power. What cost £1 in the 1970s now costs many times more, and wages have not always risen in step.

Inflation quietly erodes savings. A bank account earning 1% interest when inflation runs at 5% is losing value each year. What looks stable in numbers is shrinking in reality. For savers and investors alike, protecting wealth from inflation is one of the greatest financial challenges.

Historical Decline of the Pound

A glance at the long-term chart of sterling's purchasing power tells the story.

- **Post-war Britain:** rationing, rebuilding and government borrowing weakened the pound.

- **The 1970s:** oil shocks and industrial unrest drove inflation into double digits. Savings accounts failed to keep pace.

- **The 1990s:** inflation moderated but never disappeared, steadily reducing real value.

- **Recent years:** energy price spikes, supply chain shocks and expansionary monetary policy have reignited inflation concerns.

A pound in 1950 could buy a basket of groceries, while today it barely covers a loaf of bread. The decline is relentless, and unlike temporary market swings, inflation compounds invisibly over time.

Silver as a Hedge

Silver has long been seen as a hedge against inflation. Unlike currency, it cannot be printed at will. Its supply is limited by mining and recycling, and demand spans both investment and industry.

When inflation rises, investors seek hard assets. Silver's appeal lies in its tangibility and history as money. While it may not track inflation perfectly in the short term, over longer periods it has preserved purchasing power far better than paper currency.

For example, in the 1960s a few silver shillings could buy a pint of beer. Decades later, the silver content of those same coins is worth several pounds, still enough for a pint. Currency has declined, but the silver has retained real-world value.

The Gold-to-Silver Ratio

An important measure for understanding silver's role is the gold-to-silver ratio (GSR). This ratio shows how many ounces of silver are needed to equal one ounce of gold. Historically, it averaged around 15:1, reflecting relative scarcity. Today, it often sits between 60:1 and 100:1.

A high ratio suggests silver is undervalued compared to gold. For inflation hedging, this matters because silver offers more potential upside when the ratio eventually narrows. UK investors monitoring GSR can use it to guide decisions, sometimes shifting between metals to maximise value.

Case Study: The 1970s

The 1970s provide a clear example of silver's role during inflation. As UK inflation surged into double digits, silver prices rose dramatically. Between 1971 and 1980, silver moved from under £1 per ounce to nearly £15 at its peak.

Those who held silver through the decade preserved wealth while cash savings eroded. Even after the subsequent correction, long-term holders remained far better off than savers relying on pounds alone.

Modern Inflation Pressures

In recent years, inflation in Britain has reappeared with force. Energy bills, food prices and rent have risen faster than wages. Central banks have responded with interest rate adjustments, but the structural issues — supply chain fragility, geopolitical tensions and heavy government debt — suggest inflation may remain a persistent risk.

For stackers, this environment reinforces silver's appeal. It offers an anchor outside the financial system. Unlike digital balances or bonds, silver in your hand does not depend on central bank policy or government solvency.

Silver Versus Property and Equities

British investors often rely on property as an inflation hedge. Houses do rise in value over decades, but property is illiquid, subject to taxation and requires maintenance. Equities can outpace inflation too, yet they carry volatility tied to company performance and global markets.

Silver complements these assets. It is liquid, divisible and requires no upkeep. While it may not generate income, its role is protection. When combined with other assets, it strengthens overall inflation resilience.

Practical Inflation Protection

Using silver to guard against inflation involves discipline. A few practical steps help maximise effectiveness:

- **Buy consistently:** regular purchases build a hedge gradually.

- **Focus on liquidity:** coins like Britannias are easier to sell during inflationary spikes.

- **Keep perspective:** silver is one part of a diversified strategy, not the entire solution.

- **Avoid panic:** inflation often stirs fear. Calm accumulation beats rushed decisions.

Silver's Psychological Benefit

Beyond financial mechanics, silver provides peace of mind. Holding physical wealth that cannot be devalued by policy brings reassurance. During periods when headlines scream about rising prices, silver in the safe represents stability. This psychological comfort is as valuable as the financial protection it offers.

Conclusion of Chapter 9

Inflation is an unavoidable reality in Britain. Over decades, it has eroded the pound's purchasing power and undermined savings. Silver offers protection, not through magic, but through its permanence, scarcity and history as money.

For UK investors, stacking silver is a way to balance the uncertainty of paper currency with the stability of hard assets. While it may fluctuate in the short term, over the long haul silver has preserved wealth in the face of inflation's relentless tide.

In the next chapter we will explore **the global role of silver**, examining how international demand and supply shape prices for UK investors.

Chapter 10 – The Global Role of Silver

Silver as a Global Commodity

Although many UK investors think about silver in local terms — buying Britannias, paying VAT, or trading peer-to-peer — the price of silver is ultimately shaped by global forces. Unlike property or domestic equities, silver is a worldwide commodity. It is mined across continents, consumed by industries in Asia and North America, and traded on exchanges in London, New York and Shanghai.

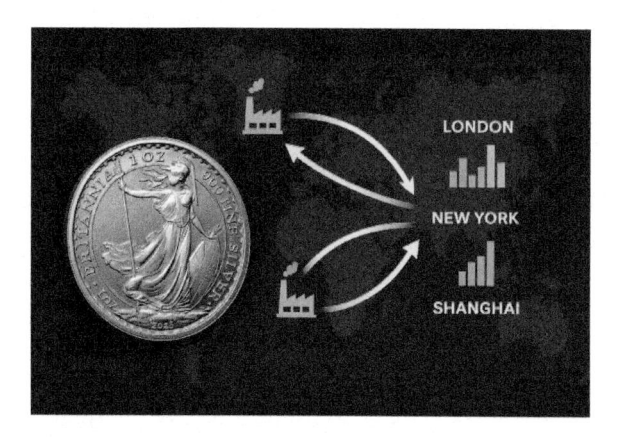

Understanding silver's global role provides valuable context. It helps explain why prices move in ways that sometimes seem disconnected from local events. It also shows how international supply and demand trends eventually filter down to every UK stacker.

Global Mining and Supply

Silver mining is geographically diverse. The largest producers include Mexico, Peru, China and Russia. Smaller but still significant output comes from Australia, the United States and Poland.

Unlike gold, most silver is mined as a by-product of other metals. Lead, zinc and copper operations often yield silver as a secondary product. This makes silver supply less responsive to its own price. Even if silver prices rise sharply, production may not increase unless the primary metal also becomes more profitable.

This by-product dynamic can lead to supply constraints. If demand surges but base metal mining slows, silver availability tightens, supporting higher prices.

Recycling

A portion of global supply comes from recycling. Old jewellery, industrial waste and photographic film once contributed heavily. Today, recycling remains important but limited by the tiny amounts of silver used in modern electronics. Much of this is uneconomical to recover.

This structural drain on supply distinguishes silver from gold. While nearly all gold ever mined is still above ground, much silver has been consumed irretrievably in industrial processes. This gradual loss supports long-term scarcity.

Industrial Demand

Silver's industrial demand is vast and growing.

- **Electronics:** from smartphones to laptops, silver's conductivity makes it indispensable.

- **Solar energy:** photovoltaic cells consume significant amounts, and the global push for renewable energy accelerates this trend.

- **Medical applications:** silver's anti-bacterial properties are used in dressings, coatings and equipment.

- **Vehicles:** electric cars, sensors and batteries rely on silver components.

China, South Korea and Japan are major consumers due to their advanced manufacturing sectors. This industrial demand underpins global prices, ensuring that silver remains valuable even if investor interest cools.

Investment Demand

While industry drives steady consumption, investment demand adds volatility. When investors fear inflation, currency weakness or financial crises, they buy silver in bulk. This sudden demand can overwhelm supply, sending prices soaring.

Global investment demand is reflected in exchange-traded funds (ETFs), bullion coins and private bars. For instance, the surge in ETF holdings during the 2008 financial crisis and again in 2020 demonstrated how quickly investors can absorb available supply.

For UK stackers, this means that international sentiment often sets the tone. A banking crisis in the United States or a currency shock in Europe can ripple through the silver market, affecting premiums and availability in Britain.

The London Bullion Market

London remains one of the world's key centres for precious metals trading. The London Bullion Market Association (LBMA) sets standards for refiners, oversees daily benchmark prices and facilitates wholesale trades.

While most retail stackers never deal directly with the LBMA, its influence shapes prices that trickle down to UK dealers. The London Fix, published twice daily, acts as a reference for contracts, and large institutions hedge or settle trades through London vaults.

This global role reinforces Britain's importance in the silver ecosystem. Even as a relatively small producer, the UK plays a central part in pricing and trade flows.

The COMEX Exchange

Across the Atlantic, the COMEX in New York is another dominant force. Futures contracts traded there heavily influence global spot prices. Speculators, hedge funds and industrial users all participate, sometimes creating large swings detached from physical supply and demand.

Critics argue that futures markets allow excessive manipulation, with paper contracts dwarfing real metal availability. Whatever the truth, COMEX activity is a major driver of daily price moves, and UK investors feel the effects.

Geopolitics and Currency

Silver's global role also makes it sensitive to geopolitics. Trade disputes, sanctions and war can disrupt supply chains. Currency movements play a constant role too. Because silver is priced globally in dollars, the strength of sterling directly affects UK prices. A weak pound means higher costs for British buyers even if the dollar price stays flat.

For example, during the 2016 Brexit referendum, sterling fell sharply against the dollar. Silver prices in pounds surged, even though the global spot price moved only modestly. For UK stackers, currency risk is as important as metal fundamentals.

Global Sentiment and Local Impact

International headlines often explain sudden changes in local availability. When American investors flood into silver, UK dealers may sell out within days. When Chinese industrial demand rises, premiums creep up even before UK buyers notice shortages.

This interconnectedness means British stackers cannot operate in isolation. A global commodity like silver moves according to worldwide trends. Staying informed about international markets helps UK investors anticipate changes at home.

Silver and Global Finance

Silver's role extends beyond industry and investment. It is also part of the wider conversation about money itself. Advocates of "sound money" see silver, alongside gold, as a hedge against reckless monetary policy worldwide. Central banks may not hoard silver as they do gold, but individuals across continents rely on it as personal protection.

In this sense, stacking in the UK is part of a global movement. Millions of people in North America, Europe and Asia quietly build personal reserves of silver, all responding to the same pressures of inflation, debt and uncertainty.

Conclusion of Chapter 10

Silver is truly a global metal. Mined largely outside Britain, consumed heavily in Asia, traded in London and New York, it reflects international dynamics. Industrial demand ensures steady value, while investment demand injects volatility. Currency shifts and geopolitical shocks add further layers of complexity.

For UK stackers, recognising silver's global role brings perspective. The price you pay for a Britannia is the product of forces stretching from Peruvian mines to Chinese factories to

American trading floors. Understanding this helps you navigate the market with confidence and patience.

In the next chapter we will examine **the risks and challenges of stacking silver**, from volatility to government policy, and how to prepare for them wisely.

Chapter 11 – Risks and Challenges of Stacking Silver

Why Acknowledge the Risks

Silver stacking is often presented as a simple, safe way to protect wealth. While silver does offer security, it is not without risks and challenges. Ignoring these realities can lead to frustration or financial strain. By acknowledging potential downsides, stackers can prepare strategies to mitigate them and keep their plans on track.

Price Volatility

Silver is famous for volatility. Prices can swing 5–10% in a single day and double or halve over a few years. This volatility is both a blessing and a curse.

For the patient stacker, dips create buying opportunities, and long-term charts show that silver retains value over decades. For the impatient or speculative investor, sudden drops can trigger panic selling.

Volatility also complicates planning. Someone who buys heavily just before a downturn may face years before breaking even. The lesson is clear: silver is not suited for those seeking instant results. Discipline and patience are essential.

Premiums and VAT

In the UK, VAT is one of the greatest challenges. At 20%, it inflates costs and delays profitability. Premiums add another layer. A Britannia may cost £6 over spot, and once VAT is added the final price can exceed £42 when spot sits below £30.

This structure means silver must rise significantly before gains appear. For long-term holders this is acceptable, but short-term traders may find frustration. The solution for many is to use the secondary market, where pre-owned silver avoids VAT. Still, it requires effort and trust to trade effectively.

Liquidity Challenges

While silver is liquid in principle, converting large amounts quickly can be less straightforward. Dealers may buy back at prices well below retail, and selling bulk on the secondary market takes time.

Smaller denominations like 1oz coins are easier to sell than kilo bars, but they carry higher premiums. Choosing the right balance of sizes is part of planning for eventual liquidation.

Counterfeit Risk

Counterfeit coins and bars are an ever-present challenge. High-quality fakes circulate, especially online. While reputable

UK dealers provide assurance, peer-to-peer trades demand caution.

Simple tests like magnet checks and pinging coins help, as do digital scales and calipers. For higher-value trades, devices like the Sigma Metalytics machine offer further reassurance. Building trust within stacking communities also reduces counterfeit risk.

Storage and Security Risks

Holding physical silver means personal responsibility. Theft, fire or simple misplacement are real threats. Safes, vaults and insurance mitigate these risks but add cost. Storing silver discreetly is as much about psychology as hardware. Loose talk about your stack undermines security faster than a weak lock.

Government Policy

Stackers must also consider the role of government policy. VAT on silver demonstrates how tax rules shape investment returns. Capital Gains Tax applies to most silver except CGT-exempt coins such as Britannias.

Future policy changes are always possible. Governments facing fiscal pressure may adjust tax regimes or regulate bullion markets more tightly. While such risks cannot be eliminated, awareness and flexibility help investors adapt.

Emotional Challenges

Beyond financial and legal concerns, silver stacking brings emotional challenges.

- **Patience:** it can feel unrewarding when prices drift sideways for years.

- **Temptation:** proofs, collectables and themed coins can lure stackers into overspending.

- **Panic:** sharp drops may test conviction.

- **Overconfidence:** surging prices can create unrealistic expectations.

Managing emotions is part of stacking. Successful investors develop calm discipline, treating silver as a long-term project rather than a short-term thrill.

Opportunity Cost

Every pound spent on silver is a pound not invested elsewhere. While silver protects wealth, it does not produce income. Property yields rent, equities may pay dividends, bonds offer interest, but silver simply sits.

This opportunity cost is not a flaw but a factor. Silver is best understood as insurance. You hope it will not be needed, but you are glad to have it when trouble comes. Holding some silver alongside other assets balances the strengths and weaknesses of each.

Practical Challenges in the UK

UK stackers face unique practical difficulties.

- **Fewer dealers compared to the United States.** Choice is more limited, and premiums can be higher.

- **Smaller community presence.** While growing, the UK stacking scene is less developed than in North America.

- **Shipping and customs post-Brexit.** Ordering from European dealers has become more complex.

These hurdles require creativity and persistence. Building relationships with trusted dealers, exploring peer groups and staying adaptable makes the difference.

Managing the Risks

The good news is that most risks can be managed.

- **Volatility:** countered by pound-cost averaging and patience.

- **Premiums and VAT:** mitigated by using the secondary market.

- **Liquidity:** eased by holding smaller coins alongside larger bars.

- **Counterfeits:** prevented by buying from trusted sources and testing purchases.

- **Storage:** secured with safes, insurance and discretion.

- **Policy risk:** managed by keeping part of the stack in CGT-exempt coins.

- **Emotions:** controlled by sticking to a strategy.

No investment is without risk. By addressing them openly, stackers build confidence and resilience.

Conclusion of Chapter 11

Silver is not a perfect investment. It carries volatility, taxes, storage demands and opportunity costs. Yet it is precisely these challenges that underline its role. Silver is hard to fake convincingly, difficult to create out of thin air and universally recognised. It requires patience but rewards discipline.

For UK investors, acknowledging risks prevents disappointment. Instead of expecting silver to solve every financial problem, it should be viewed as one component of a balanced approach. With eyes open to the challenges, stackers can enjoy silver's strengths while sidestepping its pitfalls.

In the next chapter we will explore **tools and essentials for the UK stacker**, from capsules and tubes to budget trackers and journals.

Chapter 12 – Tools and Essentials for the UK Stacker

Why Tools Matter

Silver stacking is simple in theory, but a few well-chosen tools make it easier, safer and more enjoyable. Proper equipment protects coins, streamlines organisation and helps you verify purchases. While you can stack without much more than a wallet and a safe place to store coins, investing in essentials improves the experience and preserves long-term value.

Basic Handling Tools

Silver is soft and prone to scratches or marks. Handling bullion carefully ensures it remains in good condition.

Gloves
Cotton or nitrile gloves prevent fingerprints and oils from tarnishing surfaces. For proofs and collectables, gloves are essential. For bullion coins or bars, many stackers handle with bare hands, but gloves are recommended when possible.

Tweezers or Coin Tongs
For very small pieces, such as fractional coins or grams, precision tools reduce accidental drops or scratches.

Protective Storage

Protecting silver from tarnish, scratches and damage is one of the most important aspects of stacking.

Coin Capsules
Clear plastic capsules seal individual coins. They protect against air, moisture and scratches while keeping coins visible. Britannias, Maples and Eagles all fit standard capsule sizes.

Tubes
For bulk storage of 1oz coins, tubes are efficient. A tube of 25 Britannias, for example, is easy to stack, protects edges and keeps coins organised.

Monster Boxes
For serious stackers, mint-issued monster boxes hold 500 coins in sealed tubes. They provide long-term storage and are valued by dealers when reselling.

Bar Packaging
Most minted bars come sealed in assay cards. Keep them intact, as removing them reduces resale value. Cast bars can be stored in protective sleeves or cloth pouches.

Organisation and Tracking

As stacks grow, organisation becomes essential.

Inventory Spreadsheets
A simple spreadsheet tracks coin types, weights, costs and purchase dates. Over time, this record shows average cost per ounce and supports planning.

Stacking Journals
Some prefer physical journals to log purchases, goals and reflections. Writing by hand makes the process more personal and enjoyable.

Labelling Systems
Tubes labelled with purchase dates and prices help track specific batches. This is especially useful when selling, as it identifies cost basis.

Verification Tools

Verifying authenticity is part of responsible stacking.

Digital Scales
Accurate to 0.01g, scales confirm weight. A 1oz coin should weigh 31.1g with very little tolerance.

Callipers
These measure diameter and thickness, checking against official specifications.

Magnifying Glass or Loupe
A loupe reveals fine detail, helping to spot poor quality fakes or wear.

Magnets
A strong neodymium magnet checks for non-silver metals. The slide test, where a magnet drifts slowly down a tilted coin, is a popular method.

Ping Test Apps
Smartphone apps analyse the distinctive ring of silver when tapped. Comparing to reference frequencies confirms authenticity.

Advanced Devices
For larger stacks, machines like Sigma Metalytics analysers give fast, reliable confirmation. While costly, they offer peace of mind for frequent secondary market trades.

Storage and Security Essentials

Safes
A quality safe is fundamental. Choose one that is fire-resistant, heavy and bolted down. Safes should be discreet, ideally hidden from casual view.

Silica Gel Packs
Moisture accelerates tarnish. Silica packs inside safes or boxes absorb humidity, protecting silver.

Anti-Tarnish Strips
Placed in capsules, tubes or boxes, these slow down tarnish by neutralising sulphur compounds in the air.

Insurance Documents
Keep receipts, photos and certificates organised. Store digital copies securely, away from the physical stack.

Community and Networking Tools

Being part of a stacking community offers tools of another kind.

- **Peer groups and forums** provide access to knowledge and secondary market deals.

- **Events and fairs** allow hands-on learning and relationship-building.

- **Channels and videos** from stackers offer demonstrations of tools in use.

Learning from others reduces mistakes and accelerates confidence.

Budgeting and Financial Tools

Stacking without a budget quickly leads to overspending. A few financial tools keep the process disciplined.

Budget Apps

Tracking income and expenses ensures silver purchases remain affordable. Apps that categorise spending reveal space for stacking without strain.

Automatic Transfers

Some set up monthly transfers into a separate account earmarked for silver. This creates consistency and removes the temptation to skip months.

Comparison Sites

Checking multiple dealers for prices before buying ensures you capture the best deal on the day.

Optional Extras

Not all tools are essential, but some add enjoyment.

- **Display cases:** for collectors who enjoy showing pieces.

- **Photography setups:** simple light boxes create clear images for selling online.

- **Educational books:** beyond this guide, other resources deepen understanding.

Optional extras should never overshadow the fundamentals of secure storage and disciplined purchasing, but they enhance the hobby side of stacking.

Building Your Toolkit Gradually

There is no need to buy every tool at once. Start with a safe, capsules and a spreadsheet. Add scales and callipers when you begin trading peer-to-peer. Consider advanced devices only when your stack reaches a level where reassurance justifies the cost.

The best toolkit is the one you use consistently. Fancy equipment left in a drawer does little good. Choose tools that fit your habits and goals.

Conclusion of Chapter 12

Tools and essentials transform stacking from a loose collection into a disciplined pursuit. Protective storage preserves condition, verification tools provide confidence, and organisational systems keep everything clear. Safes, capsules and scales may not be glamorous, but they are the foundation of responsible stacking.

With the right toolkit, UK investors can protect their silver, trade with confidence and enjoy the process. Stacking is more than buying metal — it is building a system that lasts for decades.

In the next chapter we will explore **the stacking community and how to connect with others**, from local meets to online groups.

Chapter 13 – Community and Networking

Why Community Matters

Stacking silver can seem like a solitary pursuit. Coins arrive in discreet parcels, bars rest quietly in safes, and secrecy is often emphasised. Yet community and networking play a vital role. Connecting with fellow investors offers knowledge, reassurance and opportunities that go far beyond the metal itself.

For UK stackers, communities range from small local meet-ups to global online groups. These spaces provide education, trading opportunities and camaraderie. Engaging with others transforms stacking from a private hobby into a shared journey.

The Value of Shared Knowledge

Few investors begin stacking with complete understanding. Mistakes are common: overpaying for proofs, neglecting storage or misjudging premiums. Within communities, more experienced members share tips and lessons that help newcomers avoid pitfalls.

Discussion covers a wide spectrum: which dealers currently offer the best prices, how to spot counterfeit coins, or whether kilo bars make sense compared to tubes of Britannias. This constant exchange of knowledge sharpens decision-making and boosts confidence.

Peer-to-Peer Trading

One of the most practical benefits of community involvement is access to peer-to-peer trading. In the UK, VAT on new silver makes secondary market deals especially attractive. Within trusted groups, stackers buy and sell directly, bypassing dealer premiums and taxes.

These trades rely on reputation. Members who deliver promptly and fairly build trust, while those who cut corners are quickly exposed. Over time, regular participants establish strong networks where deals flow smoothly and risk is minimised.

Local Meets and Coin Fairs

While much community activity happens online, in-person gatherings have their own value. Coin fairs across the UK bring dealers, collectors and stackers together under one roof. Attending such events allows you to handle silver, compare prices and build relationships with dealers.

Local meet-ups, though less common, provide opportunities for like-minded individuals to share knowledge and sometimes trade directly. Meeting in safe, neutral locations such as cafes or community halls ensures security while still enjoying face-to-face interaction.

Online Communities

Digital platforms have transformed silver stacking into a global conversation. Forums, YouTube channels and Discord groups connect UK investors with peers worldwide.

- **YouTube channels:** I often turn to YouTube for educational content, with videos ranging from coin unboxings to explorations of monetary history. There are plenty of great stacking channels out there sharing insights and encouragement — including my own, 365 Days of Silver.

- **Discord and forums:** real-time discussions enable quick sharing of price updates, dealer deals and trading opportunities. Stackers Social, for instance, brings together precious metals enthusiasts from around the world, with a marketplace for peer-to-peer trading.

- **Social media groups:** while less specialised, platforms like Facebook and Reddit host active bullion communities, though moderation quality varies.

These spaces offer instant connection and a sense of belonging. For many stackers, online networks provide daily motivation to stay disciplined.

Building Trust and Reputation

Trust is the currency of stacking communities. Whether online or in person, members value honesty and reliability. Completing trades smoothly, sharing accurate information and treating others respectfully builds reputation. Over time, this reputation becomes as valuable as the silver itself, unlocking access to the best deals and strongest networks.

Conversely, failing to deliver on promises or spreading misinformation quickly undermines credibility. Communities self-regulate by highlighting both trustworthy and untrustworthy members.

Learning Beyond Silver

Communities also broaden horizons beyond bullion. Discussions often cover related topics such as gold, platinum, economic policy or personal finance. Many stackers discover new interests or refine broader investment strategies through these conversations.

The shared mindset of preserving wealth and planning for the future creates bonds that extend past silver. Some friendships forged in stacking circles evolve into lasting personal connections.

Balancing Community and Privacy

While community is valuable, privacy remains vital. Sharing too much detail about your holdings can create security risks. Wise stackers participate actively without revealing exact amounts or storage arrangements. Using pseudonyms online and keeping personal information limited balances engagement with safety.

Conclusion of Chapter 13

Silver stacking does not have to be a lonely path. Communities provide knowledge, trust and opportunities that accelerate learning and enhance enjoyment. Peer-to-peer markets lower costs, local events foster direct connection, and online networks link UK investors to a global movement.

Whether through a YouTube channel, a Discord group or a coin fair, connecting with others transforms stacking from a private act into a shared pursuit. By blending community involvement with discretion, UK stackers gain the best of both worlds: support from peers and security at home.

In the next chapter we will explore **silver as a long-term wealth strategy**, looking at how to set realistic expectations and use silver as part of generational planning.

Chapter 14 – Silver as a Long-Term Wealth Strategy

Thinking in Decades, Not Days

Silver rewards patience. Unlike equities, which can surge on quarterly earnings, or property, which can be flipped within years, silver's strength lies in time. Its value emerges across decades as inflation erodes currency and financial cycles play out. For UK investors, silver is less about speculation and more about long-term resilience.

Approaching silver as a wealth strategy requires a shift in mindset. The goal is not to double your money overnight but to preserve and pass on purchasing power across generations.

The Role of Silver in a Portfolio

Every asset has strengths and weaknesses. Property yields rent but requires maintenance. Shares provide dividends but carry company risk. Bonds deliver income but falter during inflation. Silver contributes stability, liquidity and diversification.

A modest allocation to silver — perhaps 5–15% of total assets — provides a hedge against shocks. Unlike financial instruments, physical silver is not dependent on counterparties. It cannot be defaulted upon or hacked. It simply exists, immune to the failures of digital systems.

Intergenerational Wealth

For centuries, families across Britain preserved wealth through tangible assets: land, property, art, gold and silver. Passing down silver coins or bars continues this tradition. Unlike cash, which may devalue in storage, or digital assets, which may be forgotten with lost passwords, silver endures.

Stackers often describe their holdings as a gift to children or grandchildren. A tube of Britannias tucked away today may cover a grandchild's education costs decades later. The sentimental value of passing something physical enhances its financial role.

Setting Realistic Expectations

Silver is not a magic ticket to riches. Prices rise and fall, sometimes dramatically. For long-term strategy, expect the following:

- **Periods of frustration:** silver may drift sideways for years.

- **Sudden surges:** crises or inflation spikes can push prices rapidly higher.

- **Corrections:** after rallies, pullbacks are common.

By expecting volatility, you avoid disillusionment. The focus should be ounces accumulated, not short-term profits. Over a lifetime, silver serves as insurance, not speculation.

Building Discipline Over Years

A long-term strategy depends on steady discipline.

- **Budgeting consistently:** small monthly purchases add up over decades.

- **Avoiding distractions:** proofs, themed rounds and high-premium items are tempting but erode efficiency.

- **Storing securely:** a safe or vault ensures your legacy remains intact.

- **Recording meticulously:** inventories prevent confusion for heirs.

These habits transform silver from a hobby into a generational asset.

Silver in Times of Crisis

History shows that crises elevate silver's importance.

- **Inflationary periods:** in the 1970s, silver outpaced inflation in Britain and abroad.

- **Currency shocks:** during sterling weakness, silver priced in pounds rises, preserving local purchasing power.

- **Banking instability:** physical silver held outside the system offers security when institutions falter.

While not immune to downturns, silver often shines brightest during periods of fear and uncertainty. Holding it long term ensures you are prepared when such times arrive.

Silver and Retirement

Some UK stackers plan to use silver as part of retirement funding. Selling gradually in later years provides supplemental income, especially if inflation erodes pensions or savings.

The key is to structure holdings for liquidity. A mixture of Britannias and bars ensures flexibility. Britannias offer CGT exemption and ease of sale in small quantities, while bars provide bulk value when needed.

Blending Silver With Other Assets

No long-term strategy relies solely on silver. Instead, silver complements property, equities, cash reserves and pensions. Each asset offsets the weaknesses of the others.

- **Property** provides shelter and rental income but is illiquid.

- **Equities** generate dividends but fluctuate with markets.

- **Cash** covers short-term needs but loses value to inflation.

- **Silver** anchors the portfolio with tangible resilience.

This balanced approach ensures that no single risk undermines the entire strategy.

Silver as a Legacy of Values

Beyond financial protection, silver carries symbolic weight. Passing on a stack is not just a transfer of wealth but a lesson in discipline, foresight and independence. Children who see parents stacking learn the importance of preparing for the future.

Some families even develop rituals, such as gifting coins at birthdays or milestones. These small acts embed silver into family culture, ensuring values pass alongside ounces.

Conclusion of Chapter 14

Silver is not about quick wins. It is about patience, resilience and legacy. In the UK, where inflation, taxation and uncertainty shape financial life, silver stands as a constant. By treating it as a long-term wealth strategy, you transform simple coins and bars into generational insurance.

With realistic expectations, disciplined habits and secure storage, silver becomes more than a hedge. It becomes a statement of foresight, passed down as both wealth and wisdom.

In the next chapter we will draw the book towards its conclusion, summarising lessons and highlighting the role of community, strategy and patience in building a successful stack.

Conclusion

Looking Back

Over the course of this book, we have explored silver from every angle: its history, its role in the global market, the types of bullion available, strategies for buying and selling, methods for storage and verification, and its place in a long-term wealth plan. For UK investors, silver is not simply a shiny metal. It is a tool for protecting purchasing power, a hedge against inflation and a tangible legacy for the next generation.

The Core Lessons

Several themes emerge clearly.

- **Discipline matters most.** Buying regularly, budgeting carefully and resisting distractions build a strong stack.

- **Knowledge reduces mistakes.** Understanding premiums, VAT, CGT and storage avoids costly errors.

- **Community enriches the journey.** Learning from peers and trading directly adds both efficiency and enjoyment.

- **Silver is long term.** It is not about quick gains but about decades of preservation.

These principles apply whether you own a handful of Britannias or a vault full of bars.

Silver in a British Context

Stacking in the UK comes with unique challenges: VAT on new silver, a smaller dealer base and exposure to sterling's fluctuations. Yet British stackers also enjoy unique advantages. Britannias are CGT-exempt, the secondary market is vibrant and London remains a global hub for bullion trading. By understanding the landscape, UK investors can turn challenges into opportunities.

The Role of Community

Although stacking is personal, it is not lonely. Online groups, local fairs and stacking channels all provide connection. Among them, *365 Days of Silver* offers a wealth of insights, standing alongside many other excellent channels that educate and inspire. Stackers Social, an international Discord group for precious metal investors, provides a peer-to-peer marketplace and a community of like-minded individuals. Engaging with these resources builds confidence and camaraderie while keeping costs lower.

Patience and Perspective

Above all, stacking silver is about patience. There will be times when prices drift sideways and times when they surge. Both are part of the journey. The disciplined stacker keeps perspective, focusing not on daily swings but on long-term security.

A tube of Britannias tucked away today may seem modest. Decades later, it may cover important family expenses or provide peace of mind during turbulent times. This is the power of thinking in decades rather than days.

Moving Forward

Whether you are just beginning or already years into stacking, the path is the same: consistency, knowledge and resilience. The process may feel slow, but every ounce builds a foundation.

Continue learning, continue connecting with others and continue stacking within your means. Over time, you will find that silver is more than a metal. It is a habit, a discipline and a safeguard woven into your financial life.

Final Words

Silver is not an answer to every problem, but it is an anchor in a shifting world. By stacking steadily and wisely, UK investors place themselves in a stronger position to weather uncertainty, protect wealth and leave a legacy.

So take the lessons from this book, put them into practice and build your own path with patience and conviction. And when you seek encouragement or community, you will find it in stacking circles both online and offline — including channels like *365 Days of Silver* and groups such as Stackers Social.

Silver rewards the patient. Stay disciplined, stay secure, and let every ounce remind you that wealth preserved is wealth earned.

Appendices

Appendix A – Glossary of Key Terms

Assay – A test of a metal's purity. Minted bars are often sealed in assay cards confirming their content.

Bar – A block of refined silver, often ranging from 100g to 1kg for UK investors.

Base Metal – Metals such as copper or nickel, sometimes used in fakes or older coinage.

Beautiful Beard – Keep a look out for SyTheSoundman's fantastic beard.

Bullion – Precious metal valued for weight and purity rather than collectability.

Buy-Back Price – The price a dealer offers when purchasing silver from customers, usually below their selling price.

Capital Gains Tax (CGT) – A tax on profits from selling assets. Britannias and other UK legal tender coins are exempt.

Coin Capsule – A clear plastic case protecting individual coins from damage and tarnish.

Dealer Premium – The amount added to spot price to cover minting, overheads and profit.

Face Value – The nominal legal tender value on a coin, usually far below its bullion value.

Fineness – The measure of purity, expressed as parts per thousand (e.g. 999 = 99.9% pure silver).

Monster Box – A sealed mint box containing 500 bullion coins in tubes.

Numismatic – Collectable coins valued for rarity, design or history rather than metal content.

Ping Test – A method of checking authenticity by listening for silver's distinctive ringing tone.

Premium – The amount paid above spot price for minted or finished silver.

Proof Coin – A coin struck with polished dies and detailed finish, usually sold in presentation cases.

Rubber Duck – Cheer on your duck every Saturday on TSC's Stack Chat.

Round – A privately minted 1oz (or other size) silver piece, not legal tender.

Safe Deposit Box – A secure storage box rented from a bank or vault provider.

Secondary Market – The market for pre-owned silver, free from VAT.

Silver Punk – A popular UK silver pourer and moderator in Stackers Social.

Spot Price – The current global market price of silver per troy ounce.

Sterling Silver – An alloy of 92.5% silver, used in pre-1920 UK coins.

Tarnish – Discolouration of silver due to chemical reaction with air or moisture.

Tube – A container holding multiple bullion coins, often 25 or 20 pieces.

Troy Ounce – The standard unit of measurement for precious metals, equal to 31.1 grams.

VAT – Value Added Tax. In the UK, new silver bullion is subject to 20% VAT.

Appendix C – Resources for UK Stackers

- **Websites**

    - Chards: www.chards.co.uk

    - Atkinsons Bullion: www.atkinsonsbullion.com

    - Cardiff Gold: www.cardiffgold.co.uk

    - BullionByPost: www.bullionbypost.co.uk

    - Royal Mint: www.royalmint.com

- **Communities**

  - *365 Days of Silver* YouTube channel, alongside many other informative stacking channels.

  - Stackers Social Discord group, an international community for precious metals investors with a peer-to-peer marketplace.

- **Tools and Accessories**

  - Coin capsules and tubes: available from most bullion dealers and specialist suppliers.

  - Safes: local locksmiths or online retailers.

  - Verification devices: Sigma Metalytics machines from the UK distributor TrustiMetrix.

- **Books and Education**

  - *Silver Is Money* – Shaun Slade

  - *Rich Dad Poor Dad* – Robert Kiyosaki

  - *How to Own the World* – Andrew Craig

Closing Note

These appendices are designed as quick-reference material to complement the long-form chapters. They provide practical resources, definitions and dealer websites, ensuring the book is not only a narrative guide but also a toolkit for day-to-day stacking decisions.

Thank you very much for reading my book. I hope you enjoyed it and found it informative.

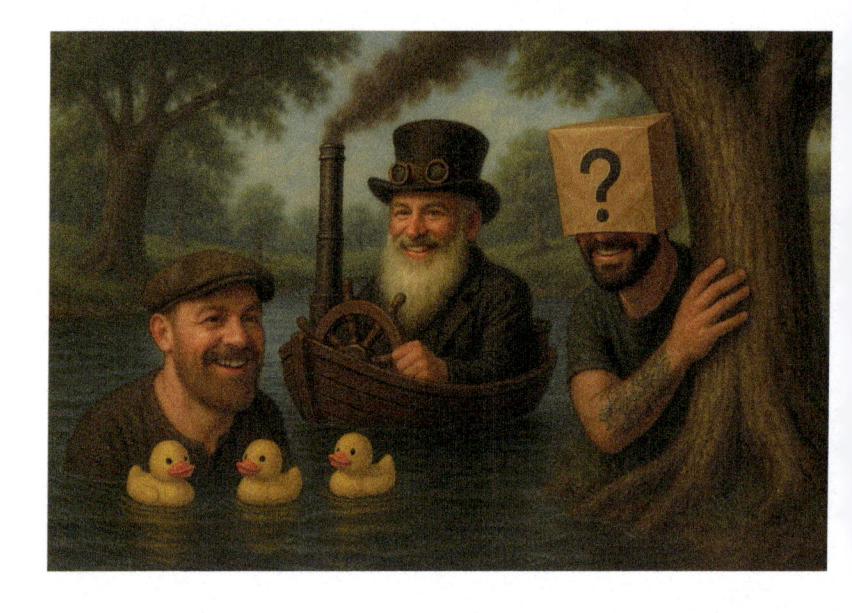